JOHN GR

BIOGRAPHY

Memoir, Timeline and Life

Achievements

June Walton

COPYRIGHT © June

Walton

All Rights Reserved

June Walton

TABLE OF CONTENT

CHILDHOOD

PERSONAL LIFE

CAREER

AWARDS

CONCLUSION

June Walton

CHILDHOOD

John Grisham was born and bred in a city located on Crowley's Ridge in the northeastern corner of the U.S. State of Arkansas. John Grisham's mother is named Wanda Grisham, and his father is John Ray Grisham. His mother was a full time housewife while his father had two occupations. He was a cotton farmer and a construction worker. Grisham was the second born of five children, and at age

June Walton

4, they relocated to Southaven, Mississippi. His mother always pushed him to study harder as they (his parents) did not have access to better education during their time. Grisham had always dreamed of being a Baseball player but later gave up after an incident during a baseball match where a Pitcher (someone who throws a beanball during a baseball game) purposely aimed a ball towards Grisham to cause him harm but missed.

June Walton

Grisham went to a public community college, Northwest Mississippi Community College, in Senatobia, Mississippi. He then went ahead to graduate from the university of agriculture and applied science (i.e. Mississippi state university) with a bachelor of science degree in Accounting. Grisham had to change schools three times before eventually getting a certificate degree. He then registered at

June Walton

Ole Miss Law, an accredited Law school within the university of Mississippi campus, to study as a Tax Lawyer. The Ole Miss Law is known as the University of Mississippi School of Law. He graduated with a Doctor of Jurisprudence and a graduate-entry professional degree in law. He later traveled to Brazil as a member of a religious group to promote its faith under the First Baptist Church in Oxford.

June Walton

However, Grisham never got too serious about going to college. Instead, Grisham turned himself into a workaholic at 16 years old. Where he started at a plant nursery, watering flowers, working for a fence crew, plumbing contractor, and as a retail sales clerk. Still, Grisham knew there was no future in those works and always regarded it as a miserable and humiliating job. At 17, he got a job on an asphalt team in Mississippi. After some

June Walton

time at work, an occurrence happened where there was a gunfight among the team he was working with.

June Walton

PERSONAL LIFE

John Grisham, a big-time baseball fan, greatly supports Mississippi State University's baseball team. He also supports little leagues baseball and softball, a non-profit organization in the US that organizes local youth baseball and softball in Oxford, Mississippi, and Charlottesville. He also has a youth baseball complex worth $3.8million.

June Walton

On the 8th of May 1981, Grisham tied the knot with Renee Jones. They then went ahead to have two children, Shea and Ty. Grisham. John Grisham currently resides in Charlottesville, making him shift his allegiance to supporting the Virginia Cavaliers. Their son Ty plays for them, and John donated approximately $1.2 million to the team. This was used in developing the baseball

June Walton

stadium popularly known as Davenport Field.

June Walton

June Walton

CAREER

A time to Kill, the first book written by Grisham was publicized in June 1998.

He had the inspiration three (3) years prior after witnessing a girl telling a jury how she was beaten and raped. The book is about a heartbroken black father who avenges his daughter's rape by shooting the men responsible for the crime on their way to the trial. The father appoints an untested lawyer to defend him, but the

June Walton

lawyer does not believe he can get him acquitted, given his race and the deliberate nature of his crimes.

Grisham wrote his second book immediately after he concluded his first in 1991 titled, Firm. The Firm is the first book of Grisham that gained wide popularity after selling 1.5million copies. The book persisted on The New York Times Best Seller list for over 4months more and is the number seventh

June Walton

bestselling novel. The Firm is about a young boy at the top of his class in Harvard law who has the most opportunity to choose a top firm but instead goes for the smaller one, not knowing it will cause him problems. However, The Firm was later made into a movie featuring Tom Cruise, where he made a whooping amount of $270million, but this was still after the launch three years after the novel.

June Walton

From 1992 to 1993, he published the second bestselling book of the year, The Pelican Brief and The Client. The Pelican Brief; was published in 1992 by Doubleday; it is the third novel he released after his first two books and was made as a film in 1993 featuring Denzel Washington. The Pelican Brief was about a young student studying Law who wrote an argument about killing two supreme

June Walton

court justices, which made the killer also target her.

The movie was said to be budgeted at $45 million. But it was known it made more than expected; the total after gathering what the movie made amounted to $195.3 million, with just $100.8 million coming from US and Canada, with $94.5 million coming from other countries, even with the fact that

June Walton

the percentage rating was 5.5 over 10 and 54% approval rating.

The Client publication date was in 1993, and it was Grisham's fourth novel, which later turned into a movie and a TV series. The movie was released a year after the novel and was directed by Joel Schumacher. Still, it was said that an American entertainment company known as Regency Enterprises gave Grisham

June Walton

$2.25 million for the privilege of the movie.

In 2003 Grisham slowed the pace at which he was producing books after he shifted his focus to another idea; with that, Grisham Published "The Summons", which claimed the top spot as the best book that year and after that, he was not stable, and produced the following books in different years; The Last Juror, The Broker. Grisham had

June Walton

already informed the people about doing something different; eventually, he decided to write legal thrillers for children. He was inspired by his daughter and hoped he could entertain the kid and give them a little about Law.

Theodore Boone was the first legal thriller he made for children. It was about a boy who gives his mates legal advice and dreams of becoming either a lawyer

June Walton

or judge, as his father was a real estate lawyer and his mother a divorce attorney.

Grisham studied Law for ten years; it was when he produced his second book that was the time, he stopped practicing Law. While he was still in Law, he became a democrat in the House of Representatives, Mississippi, and vice chairman of an election committee

June Walton

because he was not happy with the National reputation of Mississippi.

After some time, he gets too busy with his political affairs and puts more time into writing his novel, making him fallout into a committee role as a new speaker was assigned. Before he finally gave up on practicing Law, he helped a family where one of them was a railroad worker and eventually died in the process of the job, making Grisham take up this case

June Walton

and have a positive result by winning the case with an amount to be paid to his client.

June Walton

June Walton

AWARDS

Grisham received his first award in 1993 from a non-profit educational organization that recommends individuals in different fields, known as the American Academy of Achievement (or Academy of Achievement), where he bagged the Golden Plate Award. After 12 years, he received the Peggy V. Helmerich Distinguished Author Award, an American literary prize awarded

June Walton

annually to an international author. In 2007, he won the Galaxy British Lifetime Achievement Award for the best UK writer. He also won an annual book award presented by the Librarian of Congress at the national book festival, the Library of Congress Creative Achievement Award for Fiction.

From 2011-2014, he won the Harper lee prize for different works, the first being in 2011, where he won a prize for legal

June Walton

fiction, while the other was in 2014, for the same legal fiction.

June Walton

June Walton

CONCLUSION

Grisham is one of the most famous individuals shaping the world as a novelist, lawyer, and activist who loves baseball. He is on the governing body of innocence project, a non-profit legal organization committed to releasing wrongly accused individuals with DNA testing and reshaping the criminal justice system to prevent future injustice. Grisham is an influential-minded person

June Walton

who opposes the prison rates in the US and believes a whole lot should be changed. One of the Notable thing people loved about John Grisham was his novels, be they standalone or series; he never used the same characters and made sure the books were perfected before release.

June Walton

Printed in Great Britain
by Amazon